amily at Work

My Aunt Works in a Cheese Shop

By Sarah Hughes

Children's Press

New York / Sydney
Mexi... / Kong

Danbury, Connecticut

Photo Credits: Cover and all photos by Maura Boruchow
Contributing Editors: Jeri Cipriano, Jennifer Silate
Book Design: Michael DeLisio

Visit Children's Press on the Internet at:
http://publishing.grolier.com

Library of Congress Cataloging-in-Publication Data

Hughes, Sarah, 1964-
  My aunt works in a cheese shop/ by Sarah Hughes.
   p. cm. -- (My family at work)
  Includes index.
  ISBN 0-516-23177-4 (lib. bdg.) -- ISBN 0-516-29573-x (pbk.)
  1. Cheese shops--Juvenile literature. [1. Cheese shops.] I. Title.

 HD9280.A2 H84 2001
 381.45641373--dc21

                                                        00-050871

Contents

1 The Cheese Shop   6

2 People Come to the Shop   10

3 Wrapping Cheese   14

4 New Words   22

5 To Find Out More   23

6 Index   24

7 About the Author   24

Hi, my name is Alma.

This is my **aunt**.

My aunt works in a **cheese shop**.

I like to work with her.

We make pretty **baskets**.

9

People come to the shop.

This man wants to buy
a basket.

11

He also wants some cheese.

The man wants
Swiss cheese.

My aunt wraps it
for him.

15

The **customer** pays for his cheese and basket.

My aunt gives him his **change**.

17

I say good-bye to our customer.

"Thank you, come again."

VEGETABLE TERRINE $5⁹⁵ ½ lb.
DUCK GALLANTINE $6⁷⁵ ½ lb.
DUCK AL ORANGE $4⁹⁵ ½ lb.
DUCK RILLETTES $8⁹⁵ ½ lb.
VENISON $6⁷⁵ ½ lb.
FARMERS $6⁷⁵ ½ lb.
COUNTRY W/ COGNAC $4⁹⁵ ½ lb.
CRAB & RED PEPPER MOUSSE $6⁹⁵ ½ lb.
PEPPERCORN MOUSSE $5⁹⁵ ½ lb.
MOUSSE TRUFFE $5⁹⁵ ½ lb.
DUCK LIVER & PORT MOUSSE $4⁷⁵ ½ lb.

PÂTÉS & MOUSSE

19

I like working with my aunt.

21

New Words

aunt (**ant**) your mother or father's sister

baskets (**bas**-kihts) something used to hold things

change (**chaynj**) the money you get back after paying

cheese (**cheez**) a food made from milk

cheese shop (**cheez shahp**) a store where you can buy cheese

customer (**kuhs**-tuh-muhr) a person who buys things in a store

To Find Out More

Books

Extra Cheese, Please!: Mozzarella's Journey from Cow to Pizza
by Cris Peterson
Boyds Mills Press

I Like Cheese
by Robin Pickering
Children's Press

Web Site

I Love Cheese!
http://www.ilovecheese.com
This Web site has pictures and descriptions of many different types of cheeses.

Index

aunt, 4, 6, 14
16, 20

basket, 8,
10, 16

change, 16
cheese, 6, 12,
14, 16

cheese shop,
6

customer,
16, 18

About the Author

Sarah Hughes is from New York City and taught school for twelve years. She is now writing and editing children's books. In her free time she enjoys running and riding her bike.

Reading Consultants

Kris Flynn, Coordinator, Small School District Literacy, The San Diego County Office of Education

Shelly Forys, Certified Reading Recovery Specialist, W.J. Zahnow Elementary School, Waterloo, IL

Sue McAdams, Certified Reading Recovery Specialist and Literary Consultant, Dallas, TX